The Narcissist's Web

K. RASHAD

For more information, contact:
Kamallark87@gmail.com
Instagram @K__Rashad
The Narcissist's Web. by K. Rashad
May 2024
www.PinkButterflyPressllc.com

Front cover artist: ElenaShow
Back cover artist: ElenaShow
Typesetter: Aluycia Suceng

Pink Butterfly Press LLC.

Introduction

The Narcissist's Web is another beautiful work by author K. Rashad. In this book, he speaks about narcissism and invites you into the dark world and minds of narcissists through his creativity, poetry, and storytelling. He touches on everything from manipulation, emotional abuse, and the games they play, to the tactics and traps they set, shedding light on their shadowy ways and behavior. Are you eager to know who's really behind the mask? Are you finding it hard to escape the narcissist's grasp? Then, The Narcissist's Web is the ideal book for you.

If there's anything I've learned from my personal experiences, it is that you have to be careful about how much you share and who you open up to. Some people may genuinely want to get to know you, but then there are others who silently study you while they harbor cruel intentions.

I care nothing about how good of a woman you are, he thought to himself as he listened to her blab about her worth and how much she deserves, but please tell me more. How perfect is he, she thought to herself, a man who listens and is truly interested in me. But little did she know he was simply analyzing her to see how strong she was mentally, how broken she was emotionally, and inspecting every wound while taking mental notes of all of her weaknesses. And the webbing begins.

After everything she told him she'd been through, why would he turn around and hurt her, too? It made her question whether he ever cared. But his intentions from the very beginning were never to love her or be a supportive partner on this journey while she healed. Typical narcissists; he set up the bait only to reel her in; they always come off as the sweetest person, but that's until they get you. As soon as she let her guard down, he tightened up his grip and squeezed the life out of her like a boa constrictor. Squeezing every bit of self love and confidence she had left in her. "Stop, you're hurting me," she says. "But I love you," he replies. "And hurting you is the only way I know how to display my love for you."

If only she had seen
the trap sooner;
but like a hopeless fly
caught in a spider web,
it became a struggle to
free herself.

Although I could hear her cries for freedom as she struggled to break free, I could not free her. Even her friends tried to warn her about him, but she pushed them all away, thinking they were hating on her because she had finally found someone. Eventually, they stopped trying to be there for her, and I too had to distance myself because, instead of seeing that I genuinely cared for her well-being, she thought I was jealous of what they had. When a person has been a victim of years of manipulation, it's hard for them to see what everyone else sees. But one day the illusion will shatter, and by the time she wakes up, she'll be all alone, full of regrets for pushing away everyone who mattered and was right all along.

He made her believe he was all she needed and all she'd ever have. "I'm the only one who truly cares for you," he would say to her. "I'm your lover and only friend. Everyone else is the enemy. Trust and depend on me only."

First, he set the bait, manipulated her, and then isolated her. Everything's going exactly as he planned.

Can you imagine waking up every day to relive the same nightmare? It's like walking down that endless hallway. The further you move, the further the exit becomes, and then once you've reached the exit and walked through the door, you're right back where you started—an environment he made specifically for her. All other paths were blocked off, and all entries were barricaded except for one. So she can feel like there's no other way out; no matter where she runs or where she goes, she'll always be led back to him. It was a never-ending maze.

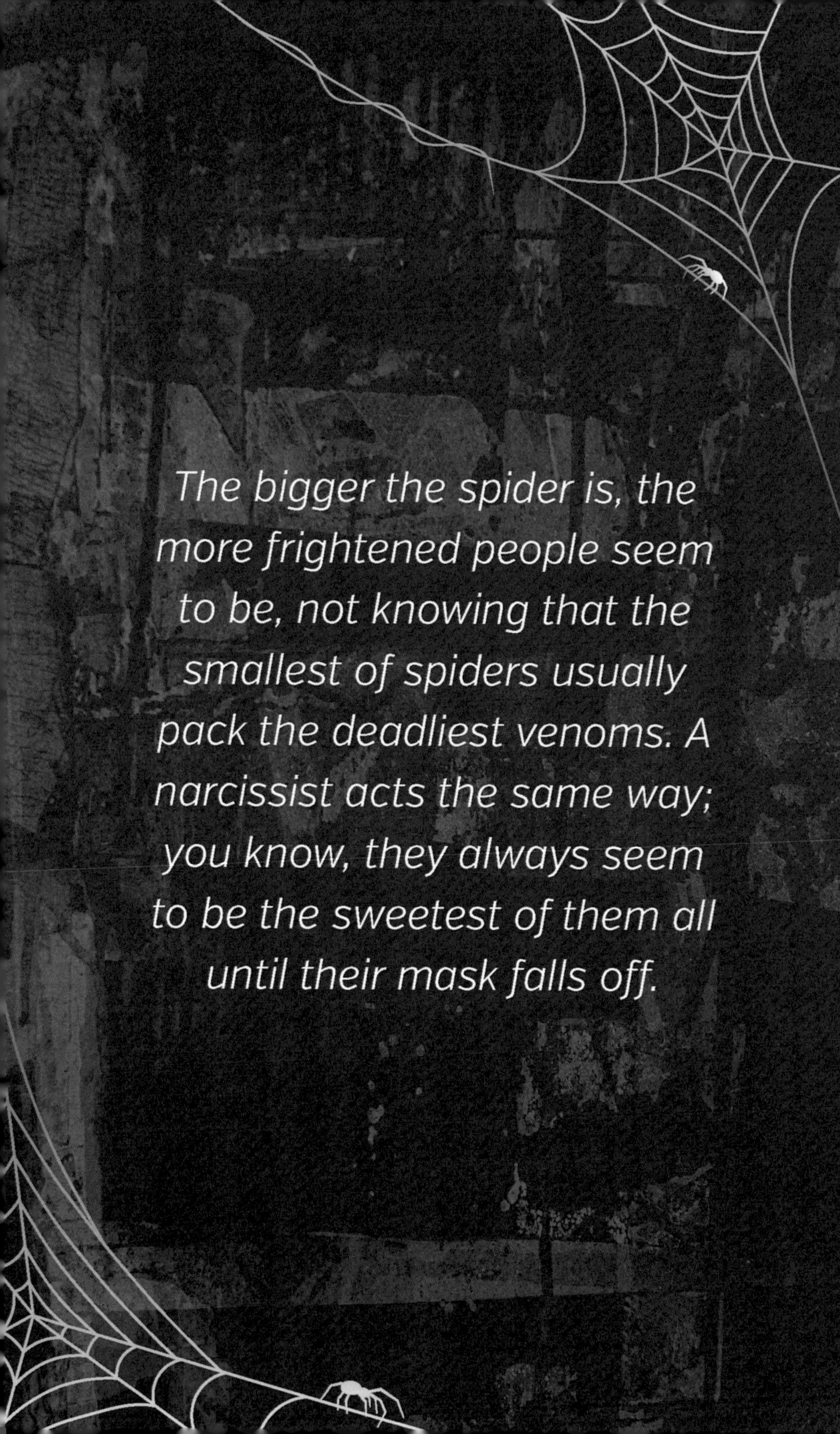

The bigger the spider is, the more frightened people seem to be, not knowing that the smallest of spiders usually pack the deadliest venoms. A narcissist acts the same way; you know, they always seem to be the sweetest of them all until their mask falls off.

I urge you to stop judging how good a person is by what you see and what they show you, and instead, start seeing them for who they are and how they make you feel. You know what they say, "Energy never lies," so even if they hide behind a mask, how you feel around them cannot be denied. Oh, how much pain I've endured by refusing to see people for who they are. Oh, how much we all suffer when we keep people from seeing our relationship for what it really is. He isn't the only one wearing a mask; she's wearing one too. Pretending that everything is perfect, too ashamed and embarrassed to show the world what she's going through.

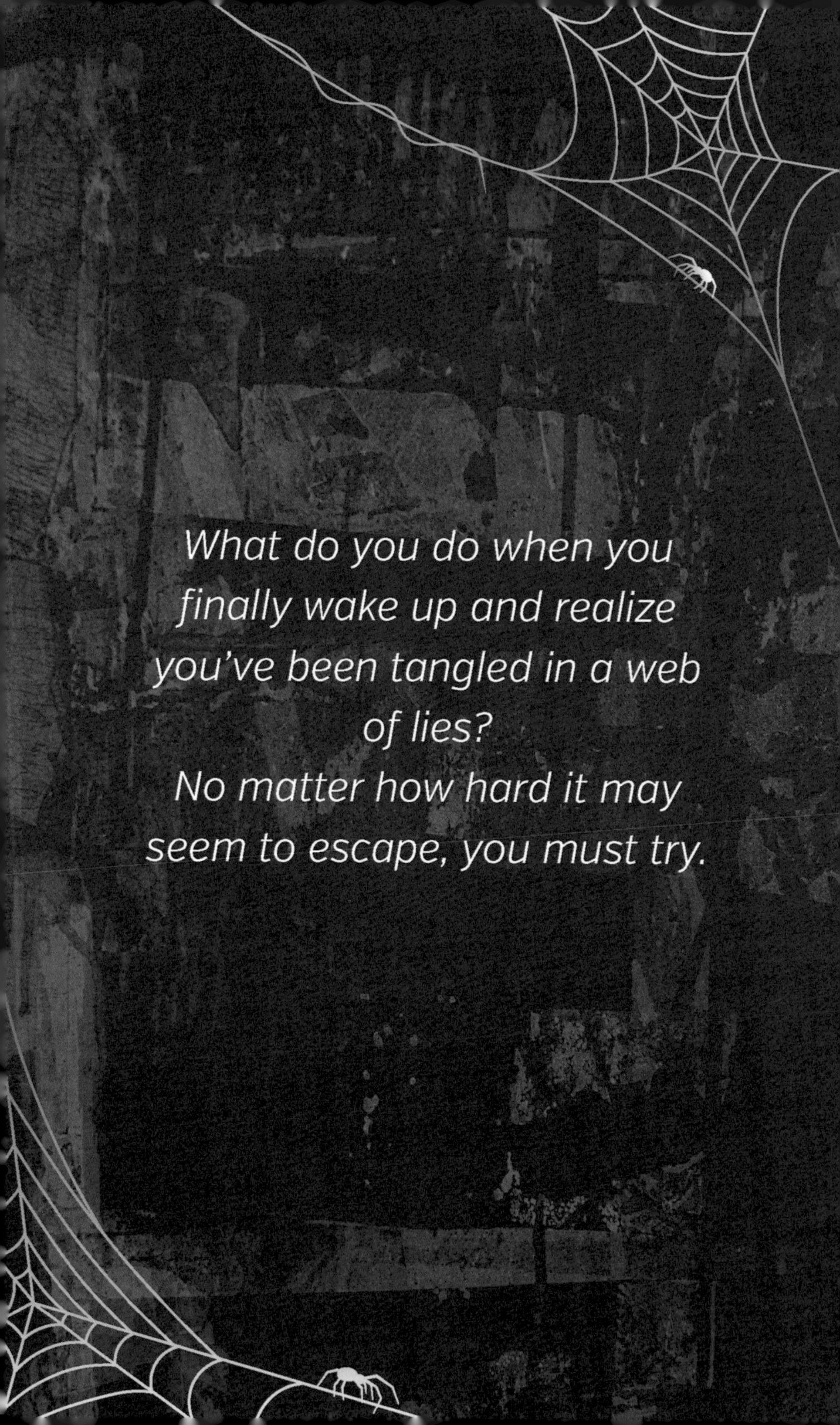

What do you do when you finally wake up and realize you've been tangled in a web of lies?
No matter how hard it may seem to escape, you must try.

In a small corner down in the basement, behind the bookshelf is where he kept his victims. Well-preserved, not entirely dead, but barely alive. He was very proud of his supplies, like trophies won from a competition. She's not the only one. Trust me, there were others before her, and there'll be others after her. One person isn't enough. One person will never be enough. You'll only end up breaking your heart trying to win their heart over. It doesn't matter how loyal you are to them or how much you do for them. You'll never be enough. You'll always be another pawn in the boundless games they play.

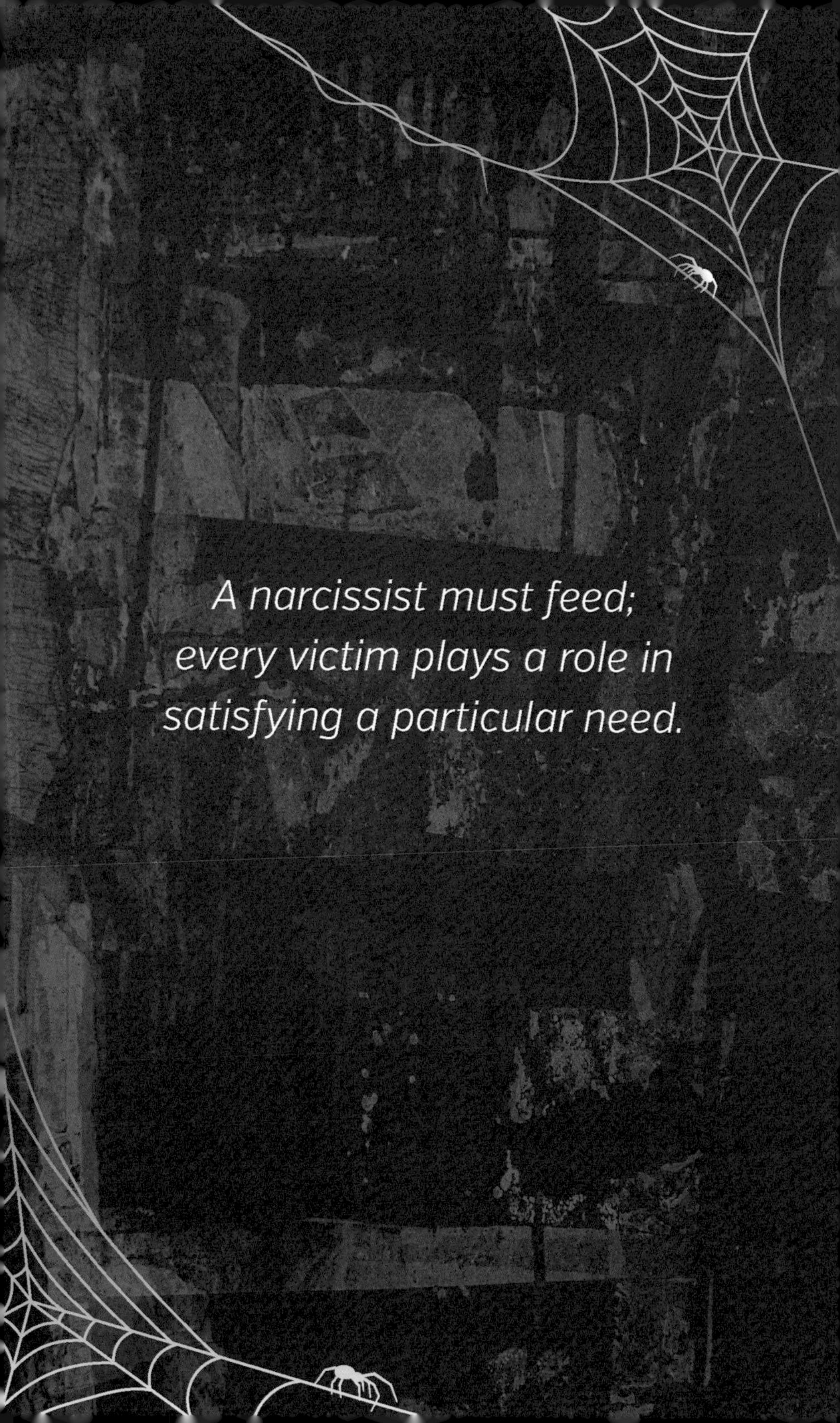
A narcissist must feed;
every victim plays a role in
satisfying a particular need.

That's why it's essential to pay attention to why people stick around, hold onto you, and always find a way to sneak back into your life. If the reason were love, they would've never left in the first place. They won't keep a tight grip on you. They would respect and not neglect your feelings, and let you move on in peace. It isn't the fear of losing you. It's more about the benefits that come with losing you. When you think you've freed yourself, they'll find some way to get back in, ensuring you always choose them and never yourself or others. You have to not only know your place in life, but also know your place in people's lives, because you might be somewhere you're not supposed to be.

They've mastered the game, and the only way to beat them at their own game is not to play it at all

– K. Rashad "Love Isn't Constant Pain."

Anyone can become a victim; don't ever think that you're too good or too wise because a narcissist is highly intelligent; they are master manipulators. They don't just prey on the weak; they are not afraid to take on the strongest of prey. Their egos are big, and they have too much pride to back down; they enjoy a good challenge. By any means, they must conquer you. "Oh, you think you're too good for me? I'll show you." That's their ego talking. Before you realize it, you're strung up in their little web. Significant damage is done already, and they'll take pride in ruining you.

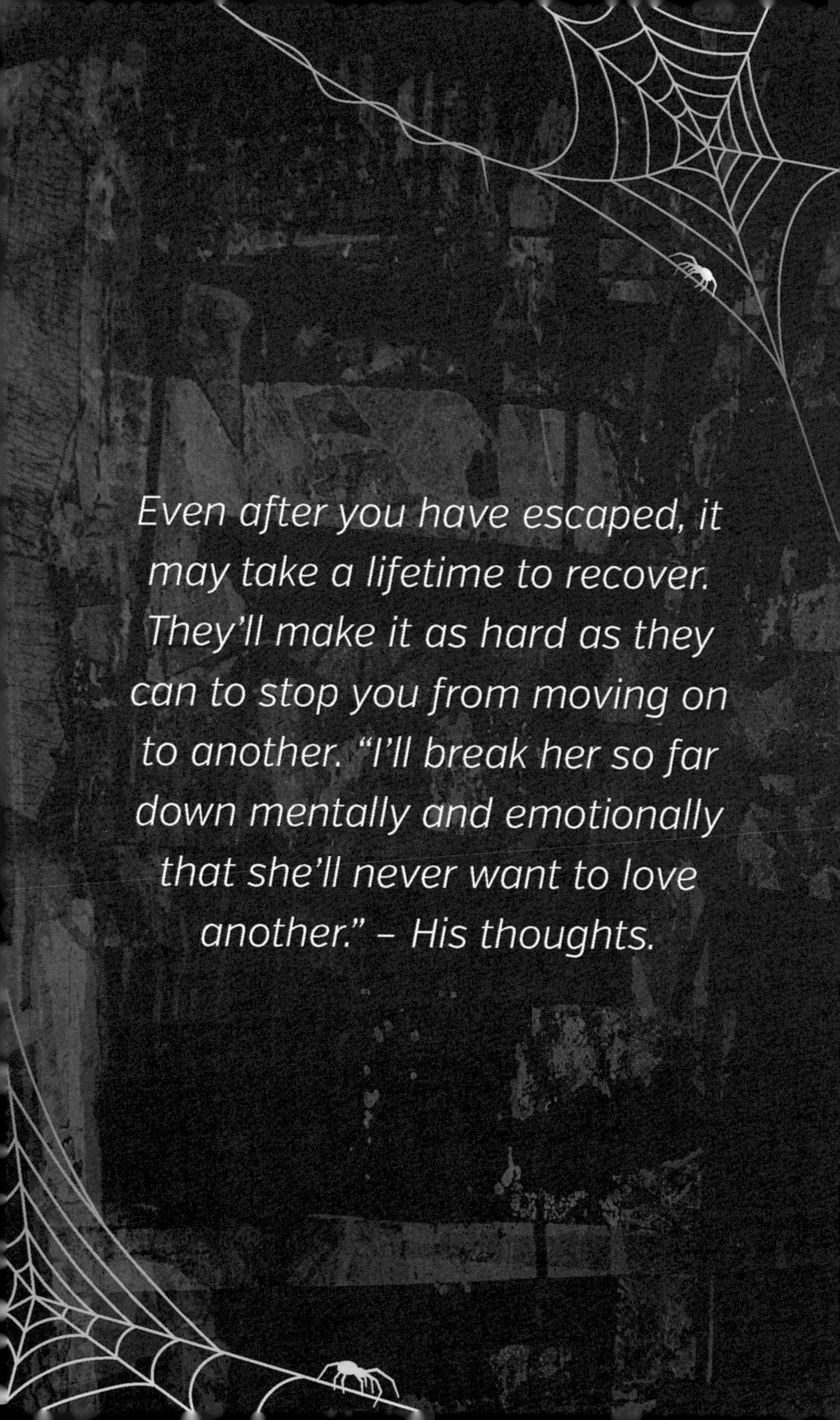
Even after you have escaped, it
may take a lifetime to recover.
They'll make it as hard as they
can to stop you from moving on
to another. "I'll break her so far
down mentally and emotionally
that she'll never want to love
another." – His thoughts.

Triggered by every memory and every time someone utters his name. After all these years, she's still shaken up by the mere thought of him. It's been so long since she has dated. Although she has healed a bit, the mental and emotional trauma she endured while being with him still lingers. That timeline of her life she wishes she could erase. The man she once saw as the perfect lover has become the boogie man who haunts her at night. She lives her life in paranoia. Unsure of whom to trust or who not to trust, what to believe or what not to believe. Potential partners she encounters she finds hard to read. It's pure torment because her soul and her heart yearn for love, but her mind fears and is terrified of love.

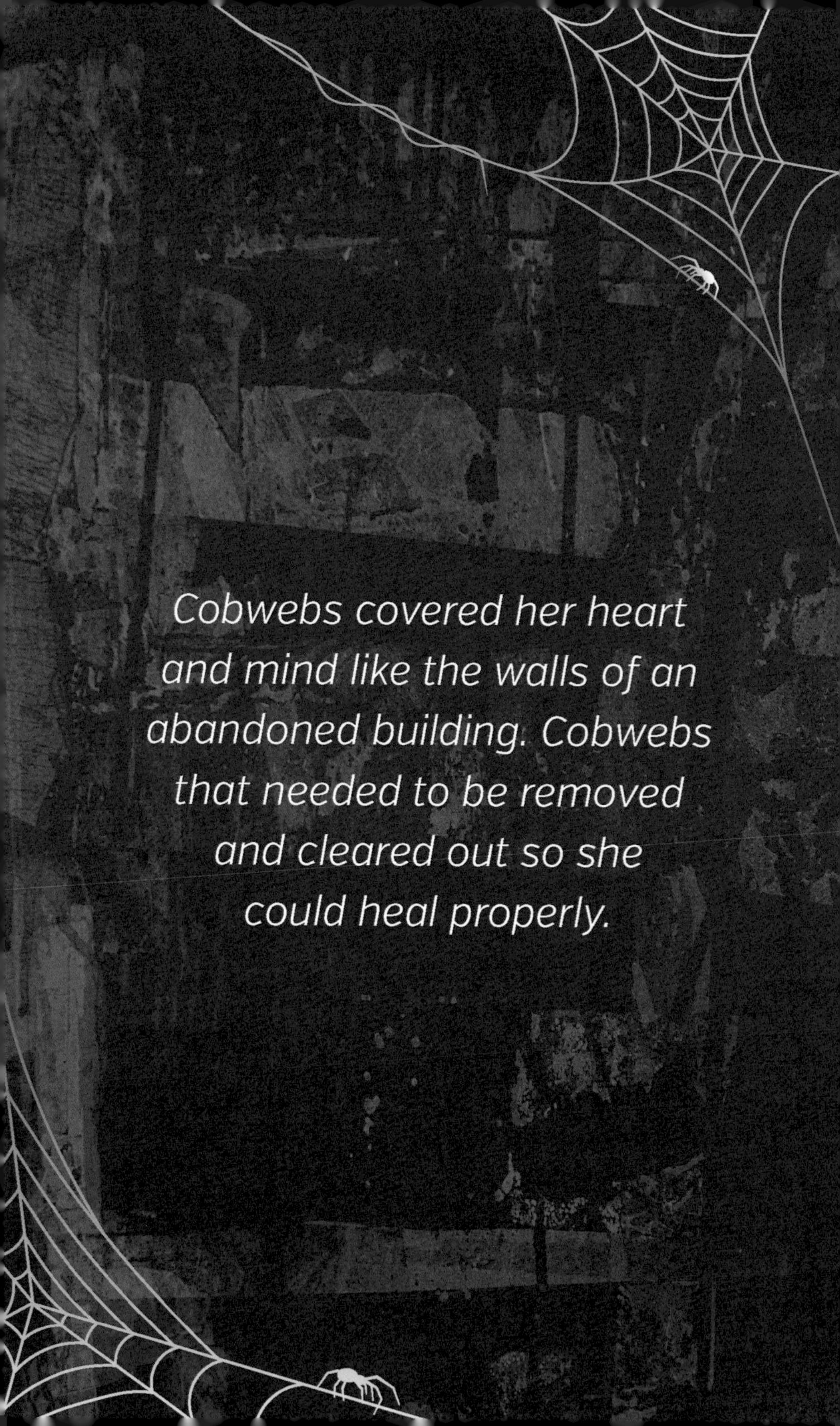

Cobwebs covered her heart and mind like the walls of an abandoned building. Cobwebs that needed to be removed and cleared out so she could heal properly.

You can close the door and lock the windows, but without healing, releasing, and cutting the cord, they'll try to sneak back in through the most minor cracks. They'll gaslight you to see how you'll react and desperately try to string you back up in their webs of manipulation. "I'm sorry, baby, I've changed; you promised you'd never leave me; I need you!" They'll say and do anything to trap you back in their little web. Love bombing is what they are famous for, but it's a tactic they use to make you lower your guard. Nothing more.

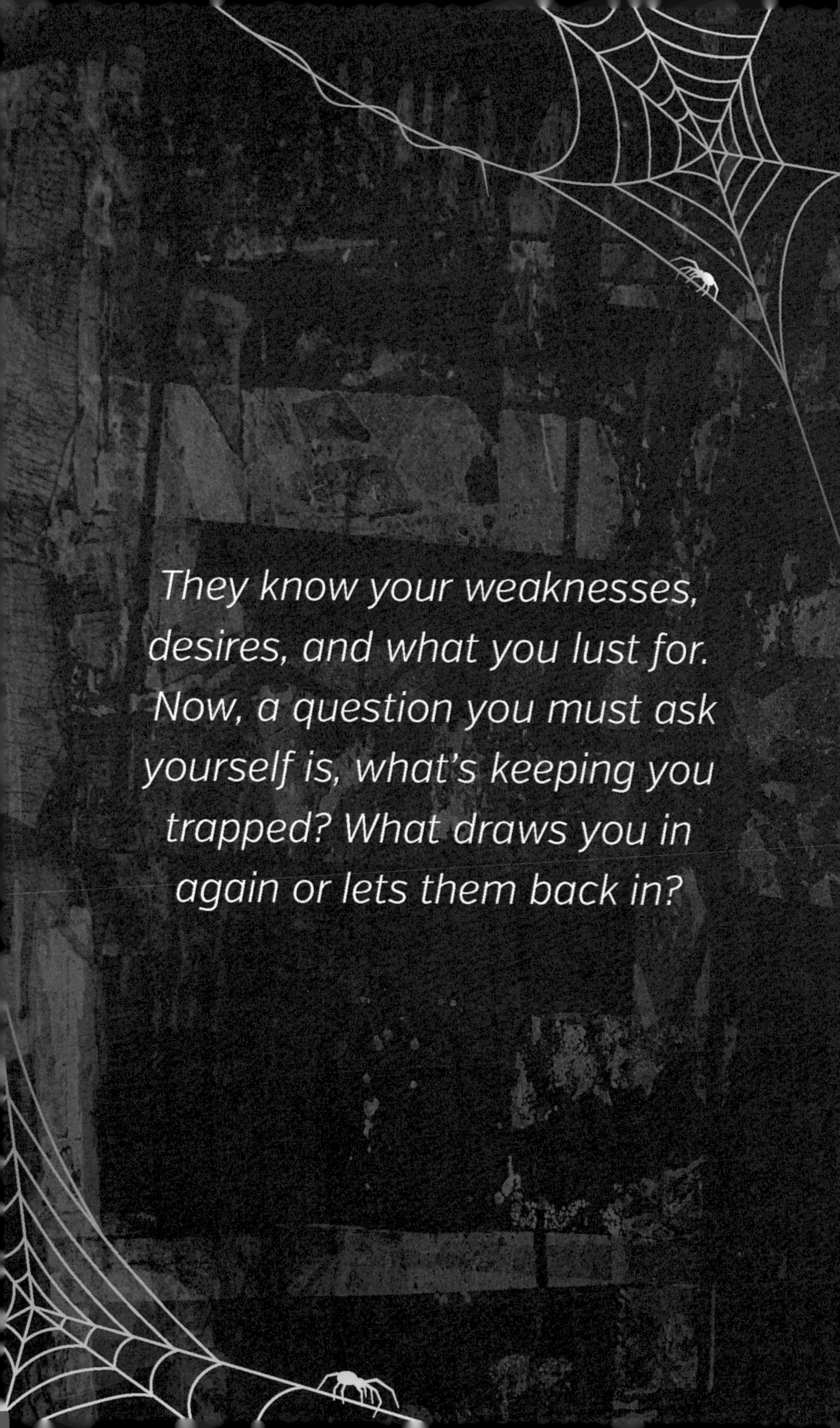

They know your weaknesses, desires, and what you lust for. Now, a question you must ask yourself is, what's keeping you trapped? What draws you in again or lets them back in?

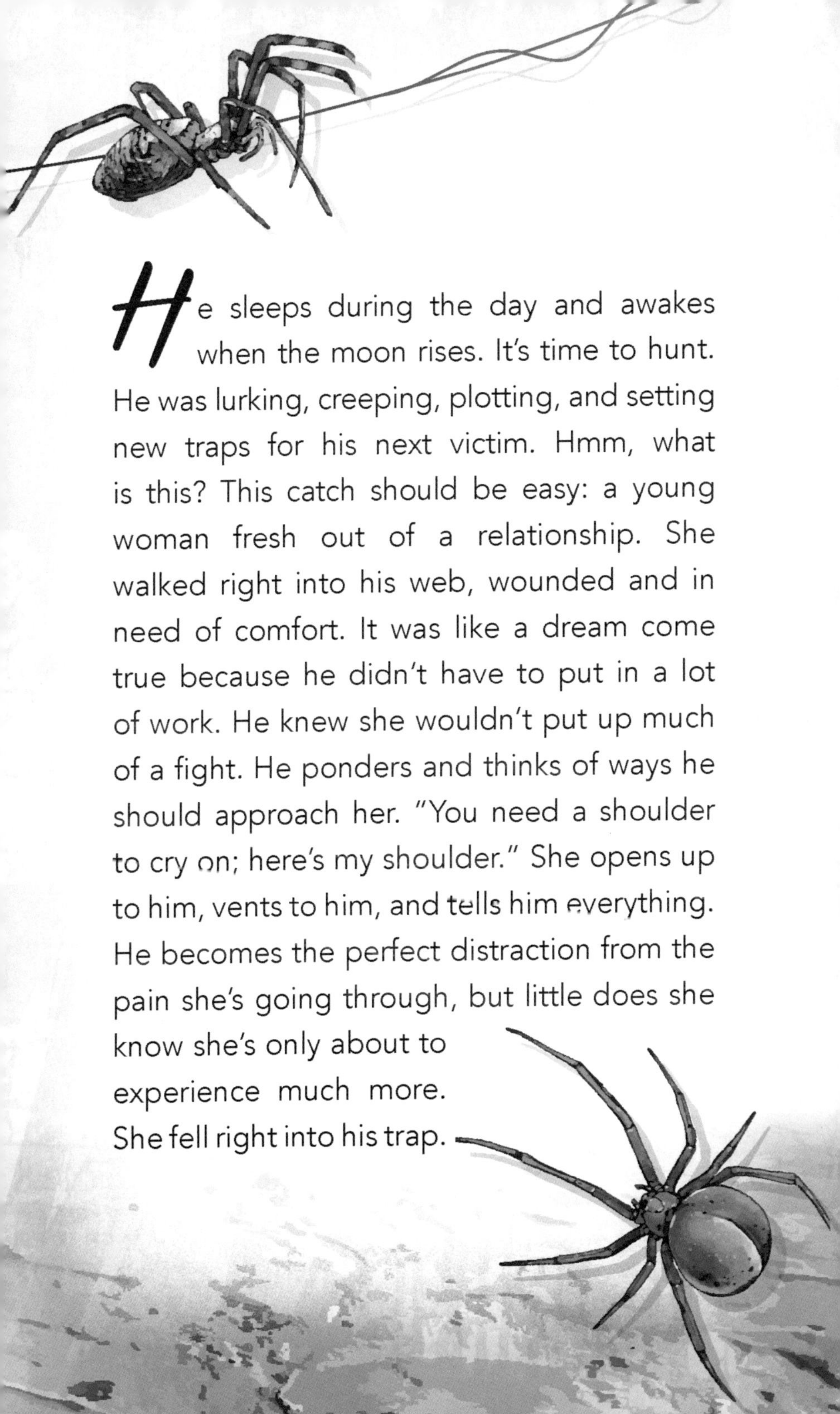

He sleeps during the day and awakes when the moon rises. It's time to hunt. He was lurking, creeping, plotting, and setting new traps for his next victim. Hmm, what is this? This catch should be easy: a young woman fresh out of a relationship. She walked right into his web, wounded and in need of comfort. It was like a dream come true because he didn't have to put in a lot of work. He knew she wouldn't put up much of a fight. He ponders and thinks of ways he should approach her. "You need a shoulder to cry on; here's my shoulder." She opens up to him, vents to him, and tells him everything. He becomes the perfect distraction from the pain she's going through, but little does she know she's only about to experience much more. She fell right into his trap.

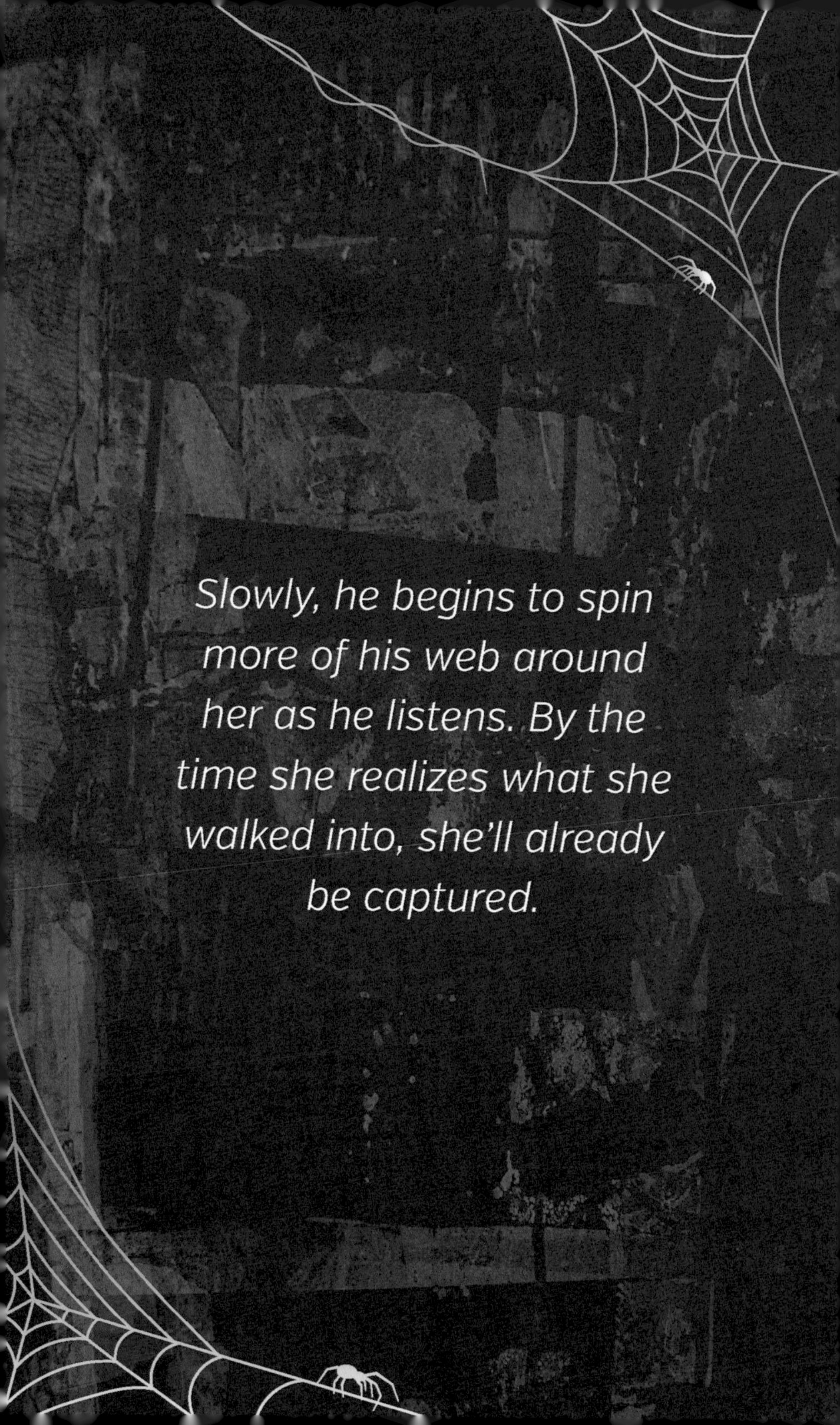

Slowly, he begins to spin more of his web around her as he listens. By the time she realizes what she walked into, she'll already be captured.

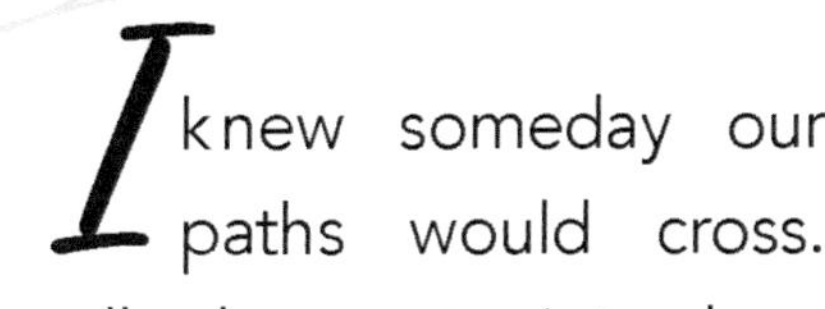

I knew someday our paths would cross. He walked over to introduce himself and said he was new to the neighborhood. "Where the hoes at," he said jokingly. I laughed with hysteria. I thought to myself I could step on him and end his life right now, but I've always had a fascination for spiders since I was a child. So, instead of stepping on him, I captured him to study him. In his mind, he saw me as his best friend, foolishly unaware of who he was dealing with, but I knew who I was dealing with. There was no spinning any webs around me. I must admit he was a cool guy; anyone who wasn't as observant as I was could never see behind the mask or unravel his true nature. I could see how easily he was able to charm his way into any woman's life. He almost had me fooled, but a fool I wasn't; still, I must say I was very impressed. They always come off well put together. He had an excellent sense of humor, very polite and well-dressed. Although I got tired of him bragging about his victims, I wasn't quite ready to release him yet.

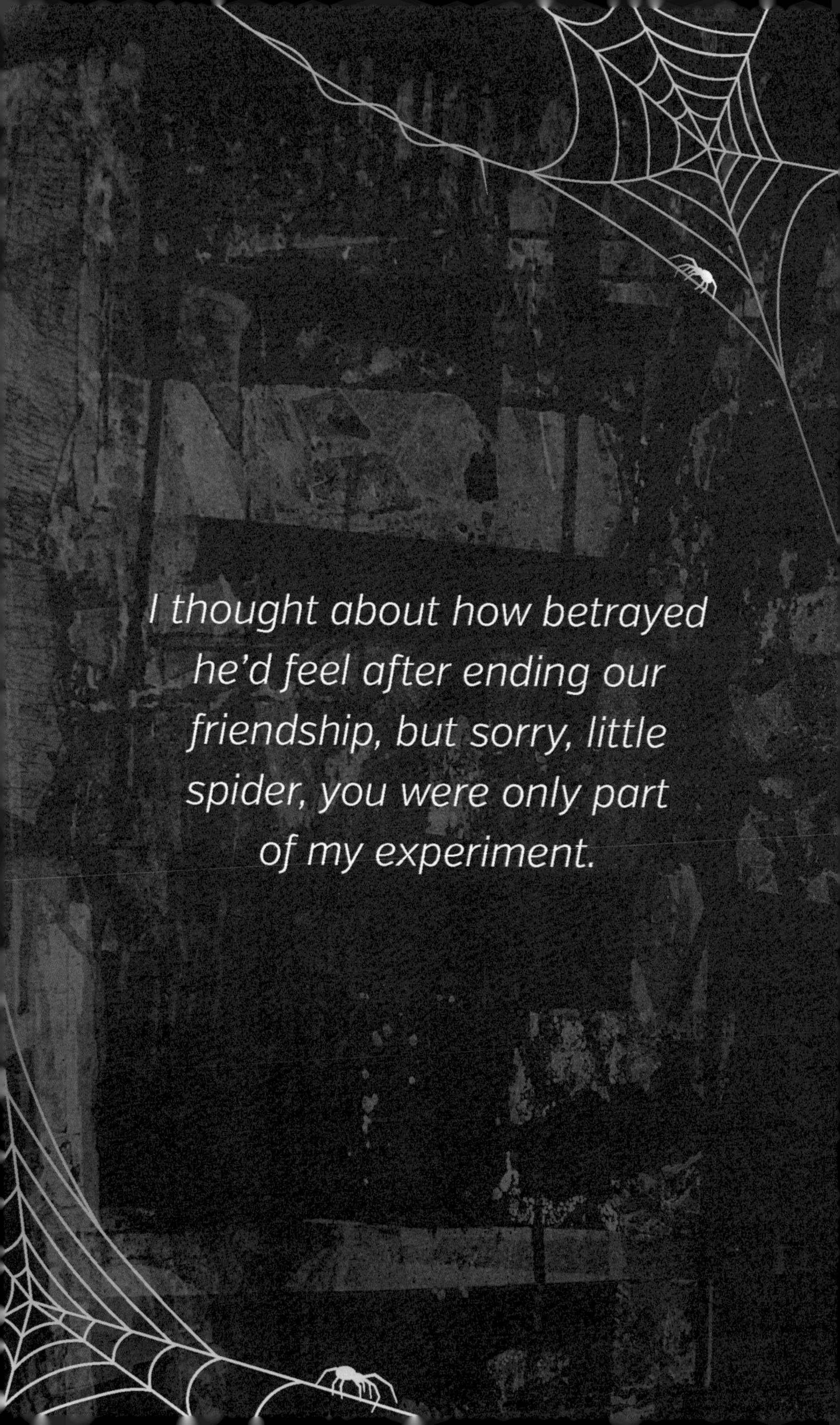

I thought about how betrayed he'd feel after ending our friendship, but sorry, little spider, you were only part of my experiment.

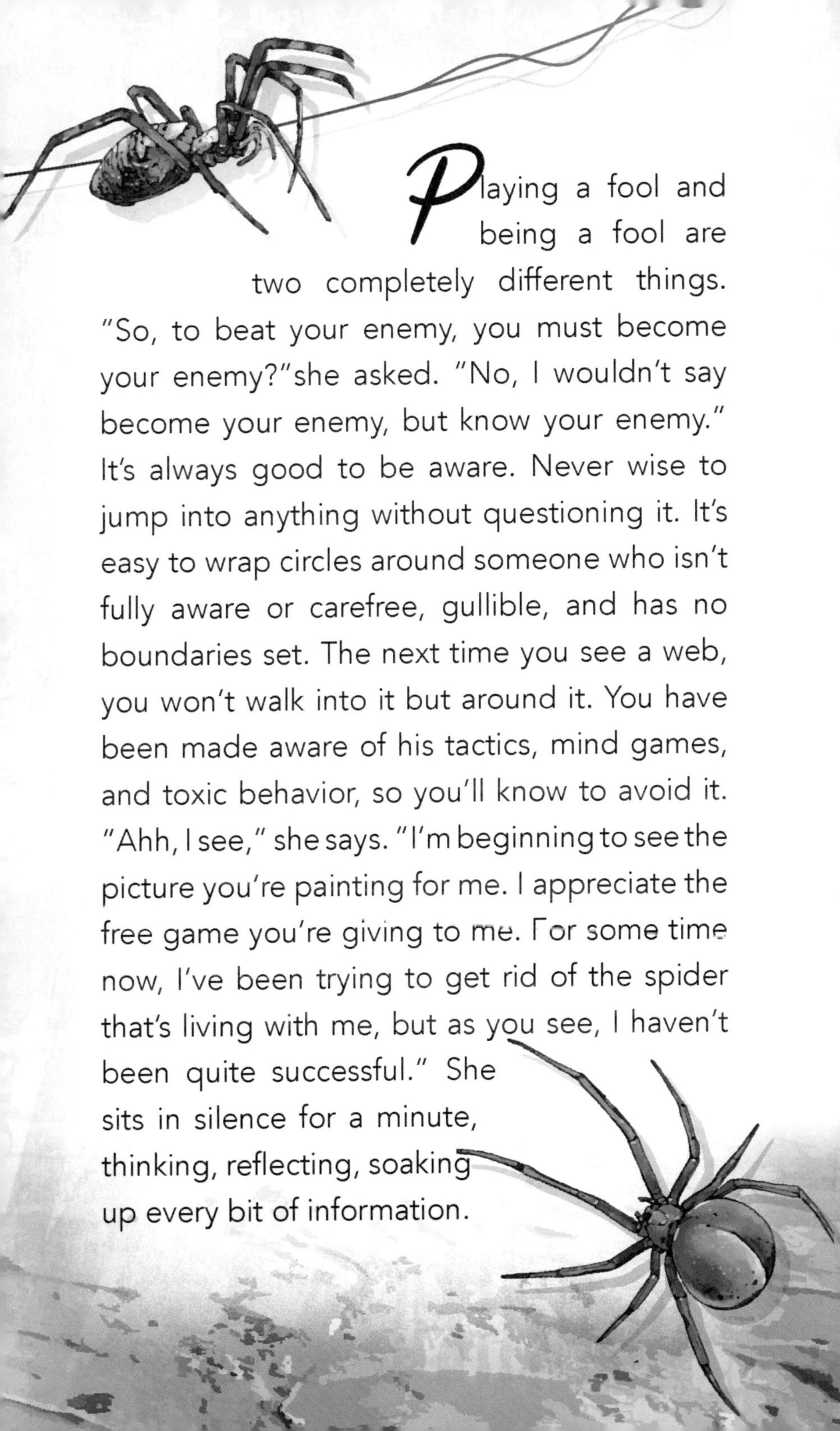

Playing a fool and being a fool are two completely different things. "So, to beat your enemy, you must become your enemy?"she asked. "No, I wouldn't say become your enemy, but know your enemy." It's always good to be aware. Never wise to jump into anything without questioning it. It's easy to wrap circles around someone who isn't fully aware or carefree, gullible, and has no boundaries set. The next time you see a web, you won't walk into it but around it. You have been made aware of his tactics, mind games, and toxic behavior, so you'll know to avoid it. "Ahh, I see," she says. "I'm beginning to see the picture you're painting for me. I appreciate the free game you're giving to me. For some time now, I've been trying to get rid of the spider that's living with me, but as you see, I haven't been quite successful." She sits in silence for a minute, thinking, reflecting, soaking up every bit of information.

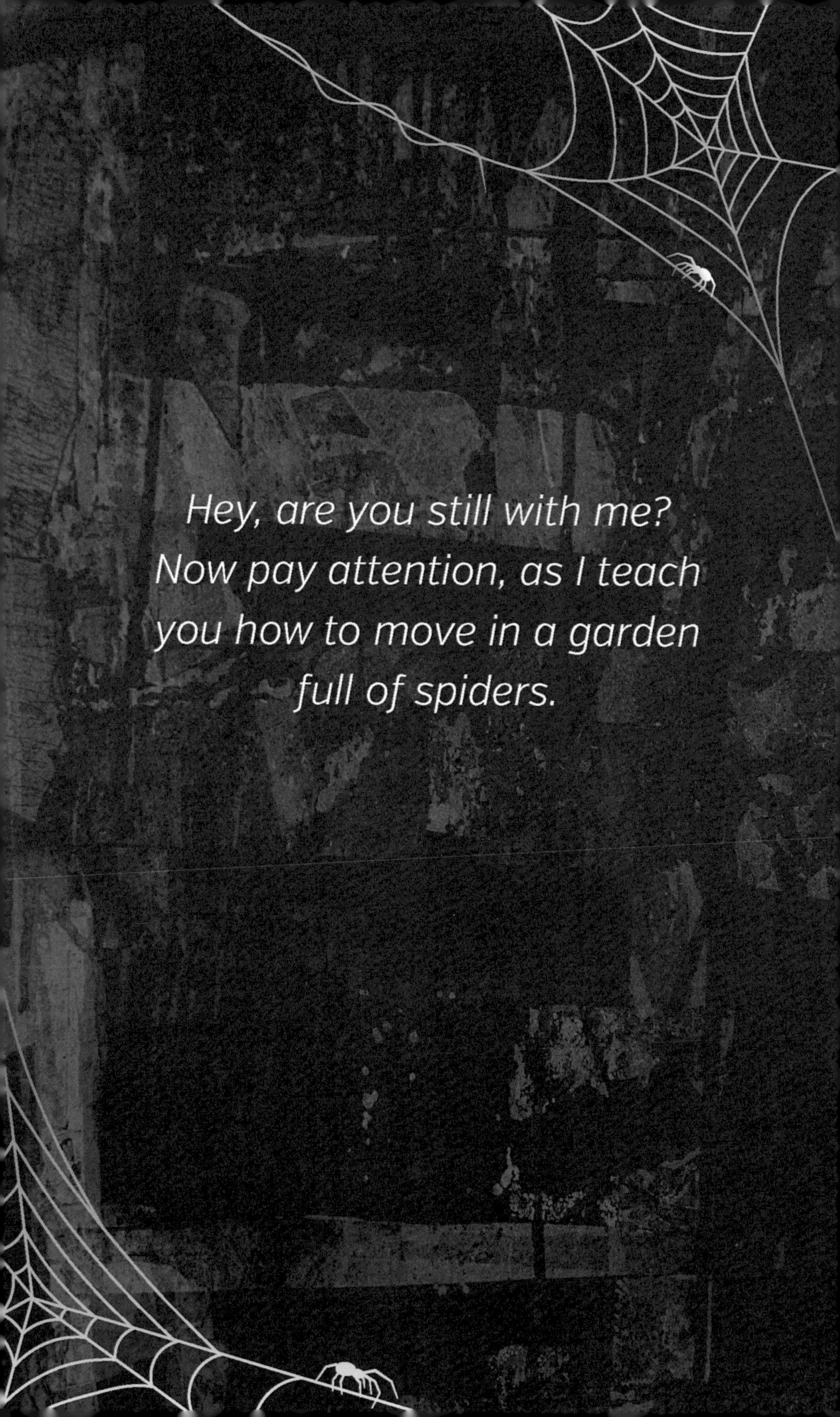

*Hey, are you still with me?
Now pay attention, as I teach
you how to move in a garden
full of spiders.*

Facing too much truth in one day can be a bit overwhelming. I decided to change the subject while she processes everything. I began to reminisce about my past encounters and experiences. I've met a few black widows in my life. So often, we speak about narcissistic men but never much about narcissistic women. Most women find it uncomfortable to discuss their narcissistic traits or even to admit that they have them. There are not enough fingers on my hands to count how many women use and abuse men mentally and emotionally on a daily basis just to get what they want. I'd be lying if I said I wasn't a victim of a few of them myself. Yeah, men become victims too, but some will never admit it because of their pride or simply because they have to withhold their "tough guy or player image." No matter how cool or how strong a man may think he is, he cannot with stand the bite of a black widow.

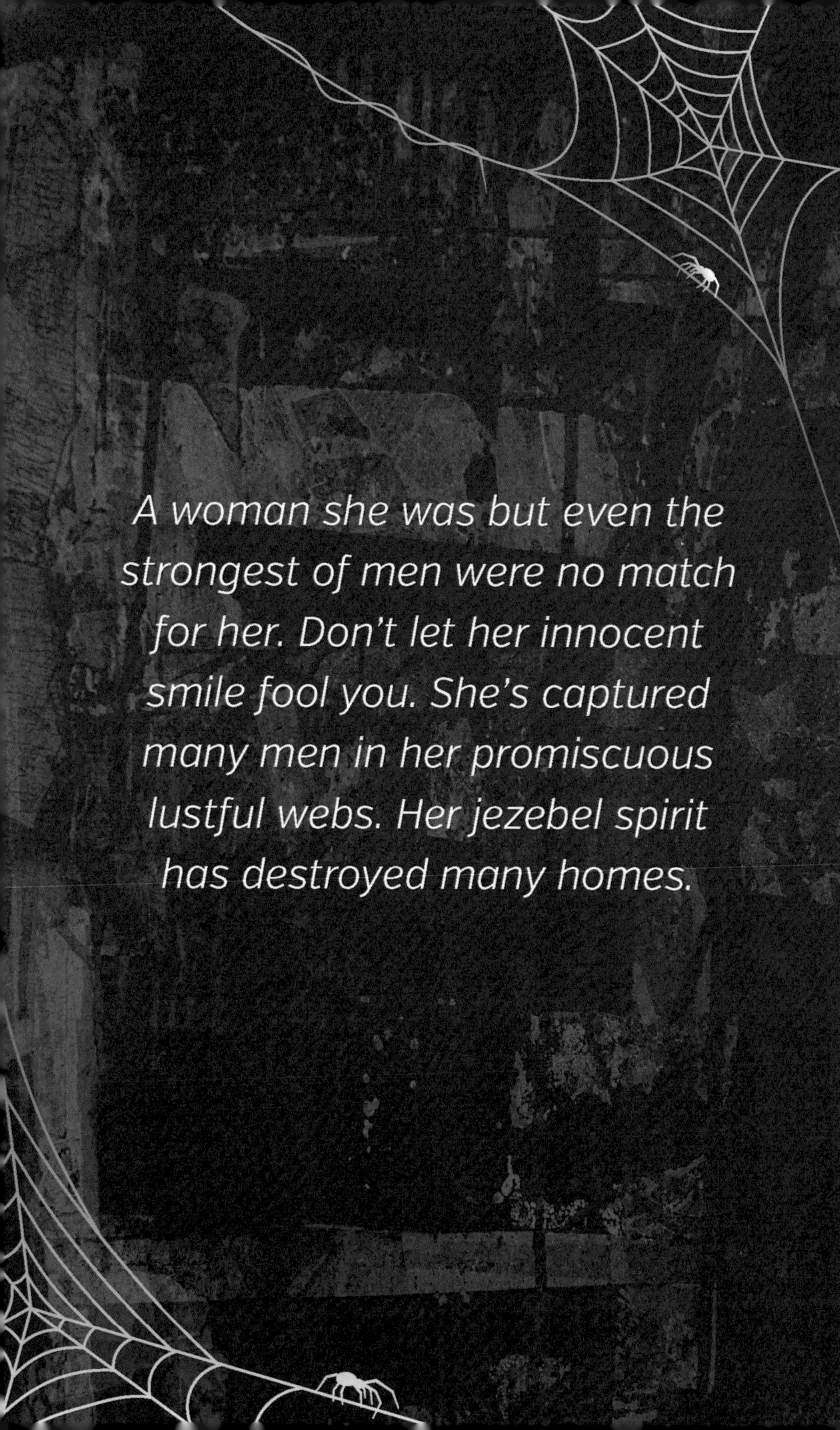

A woman she was but even the strongest of men were no match for her. Don't let her innocent smile fool you. She's captured many men in her promiscuous lustful webs. Her jezebel spirit has destroyed many homes.

It is easy to judge someone's behavior without knowing their background or upbringing. It isn't always toxic relationships. Sadly, some people suffer abuse from narcissistic parents, self-serving parents who have always put their needs before their children. The little boy who grew up watching his father juggle multiple women. The little girl who grew up watching her mother give to and love every abusive man more than her. They've both become adults who have been harnessing trauma for years, struggling to escape the webs cast over them by their parents who have never sought proper help.

They mirror the people who have hurt them in their lives. Most people want to do better, become better people, and want to heal. However, some people need help knowing where or how to start.

K. Rashad The Journey Back To Self: Take A Deep Dive Within.

The more I reflect and learn, the more I realize how unaware we all are. The more I reflect on past situationships/relationships, the more I realize how unaware I was of myself. The hardest webs to escape are the ones we've spun around ourselves. Thinking we have it all figured out, thinking we don't need any help, believing that we are not the problem, acting as if we are perfect, and there's no healing we need to do; pointing our fingers at everyone else.

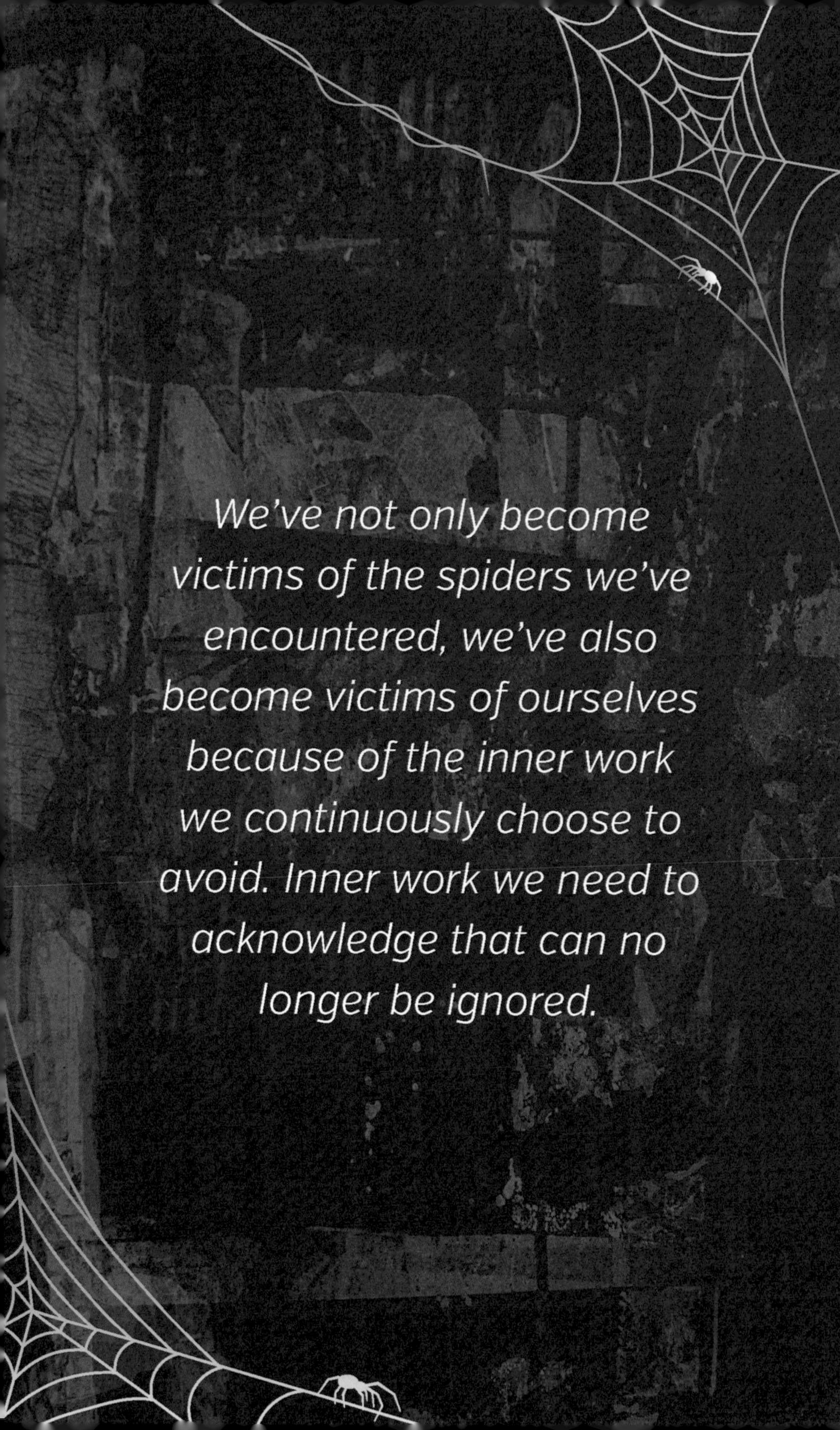

We've not only become victims of the spiders we've encountered, we've also become victims of ourselves because of the inner work we continuously choose to avoid. Inner work we need to acknowledge that can no longer be ignored.

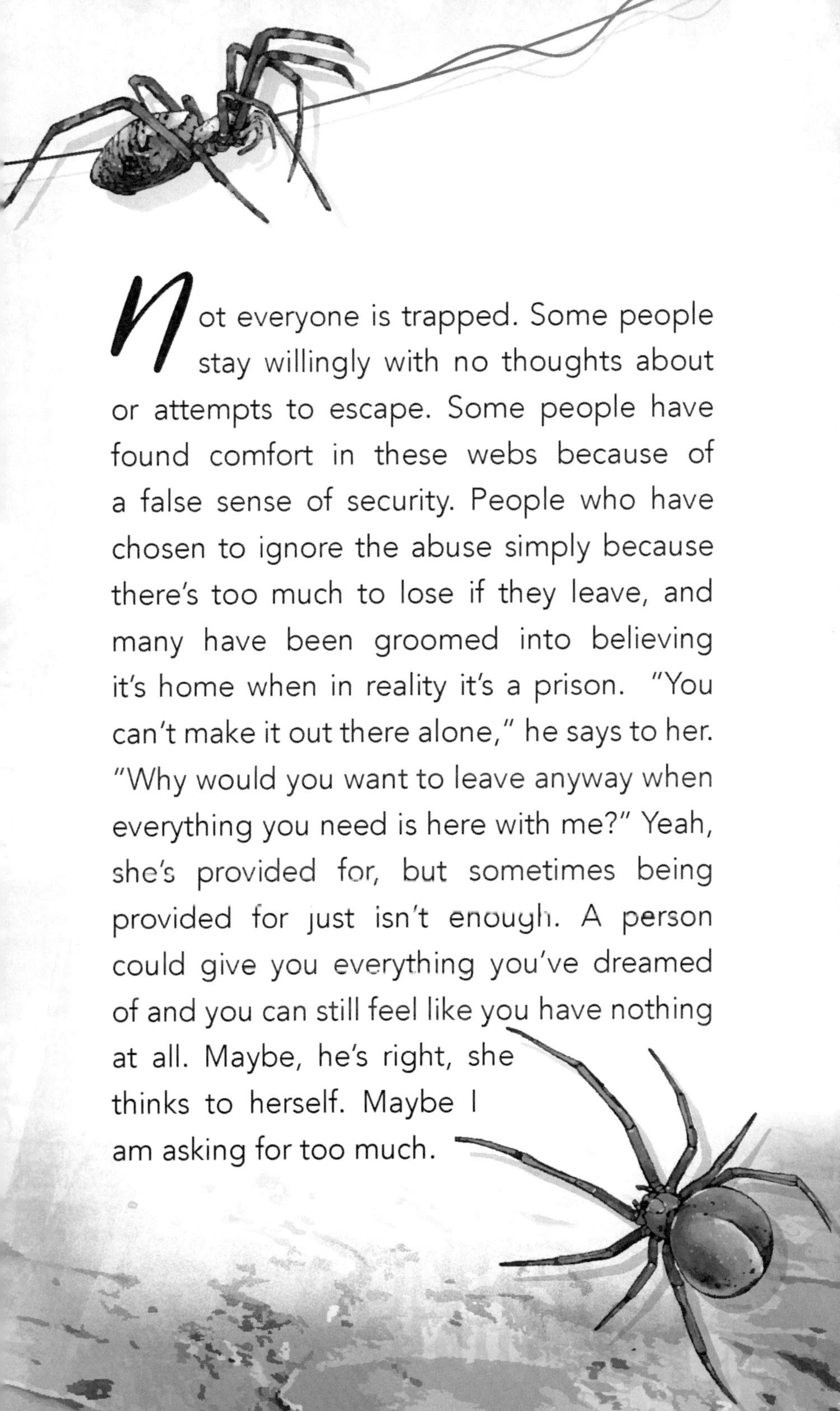

Not everyone is trapped. Some people stay willingly with no thoughts about or attempts to escape. Some people have found comfort in these webs because of a false sense of security. People who have chosen to ignore the abuse simply because there's too much to lose if they leave, and many have been groomed into believing it's home when in reality it's a prison. "You can't make it out there alone," he says to her. "Why would you want to leave anyway when everything you need is here with me?" Yeah, she's provided for, but sometimes being provided for just isn't enough. A person could give you everything you've dreamed of and you can still feel like you have nothing at all. Maybe, he's right, she thinks to herself. Maybe I am asking for too much.

"Look at this beautiful silk web he's woven for me, how could I ever leave?" – Her thoughts.

It may look and sound like it's the perfect home, but it isn't. There is no happiness, there is no peace, and you have no say. Your opinion doesn't matter, your wants and needs don't matter, and your happiness doesn't matter. All that matters is that you know your place. A narcissist will beat you down to your lowest form until you surrender and give them your power. There's no equal give and take. They don't view you as a partner they see you as their property. "You do as I say, I'm done with you when I say I'm done with you," he says to her. And that'll be the day when he has drained her for all of her essence, or grown tired or bored. When that day comes he'll secretly begin to look for his next victim.

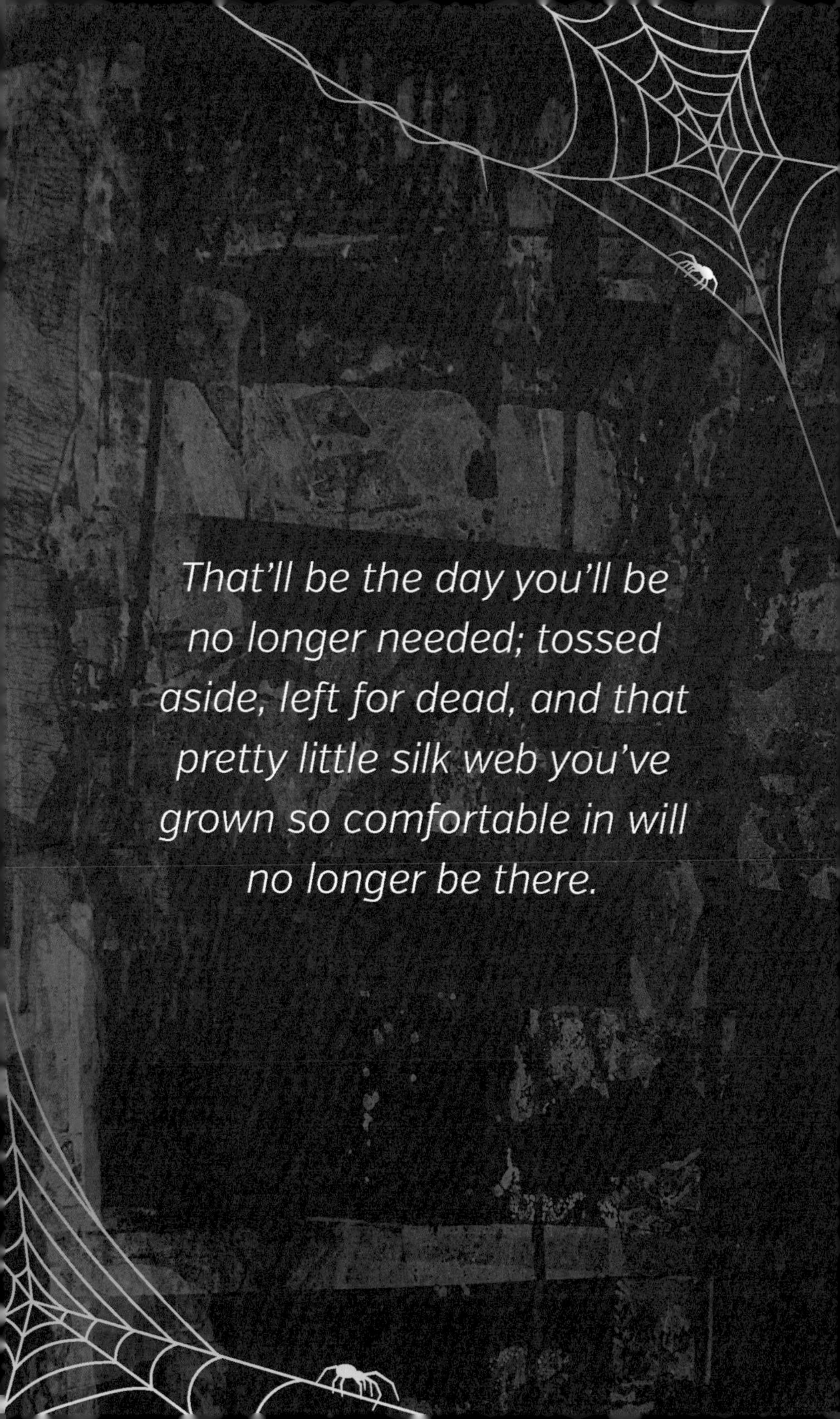
That'll be the day you'll be no longer needed; tossed aside, left for dead, and that pretty little silk web you've grown so comfortable in will no longer be there.

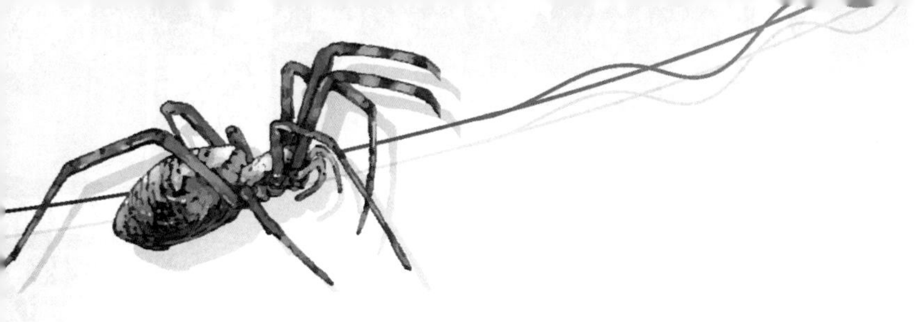

You'll be no use after all of your supply has run dry. A harsh truth it is, but in the sick mind of a narcissist that's just how it is. They are heartless, ruthless, and feel nothing; pain is all they have to give. That's why it's best to never place all of your eggs into one basket. You'll only regret it. Take heed to my warning, it's a bad investment. Keeping you comfortable is just another manipulative tactic to have you codependent on them. It's a power play; it's always about being in control. To make you feel like you can't do anything and that there's no way that you can survive without them!

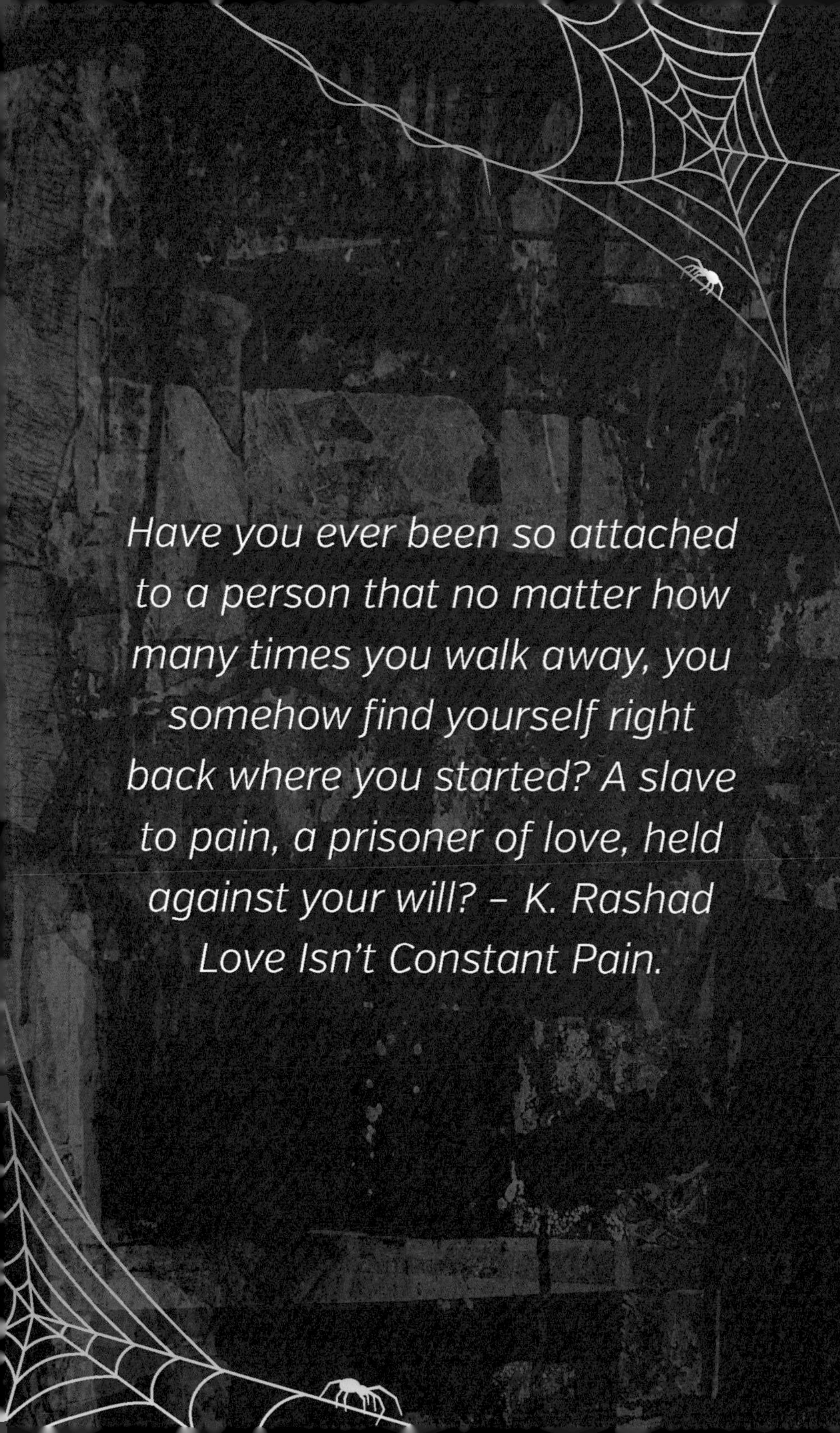
Have you ever been so attached to a person that no matter how many times you walk away, you somehow find yourself right back where you started? A slave to pain, a prisoner of love, held against your will? – K. Rashad
Love Isn't Constant Pain.

Powerless and hopeless is what we become. Caught up in a maze, we feel like we will never escape. Unhealthy soul ties are so hard to break, and toxic attachments are even harder to shake. It's a living hell, an endless nightmare, and it hurts even more when you finally wake up and realize you've been up under the narcissist's spell. Nothing about the relationship was real. It was all an illusion. Sorry to break it down to you this way, but the odds were against you from the beginning, and by the time you reached the exit to the maze, they revealed to you the greatest magic trick you've ever seen. Their true selves!

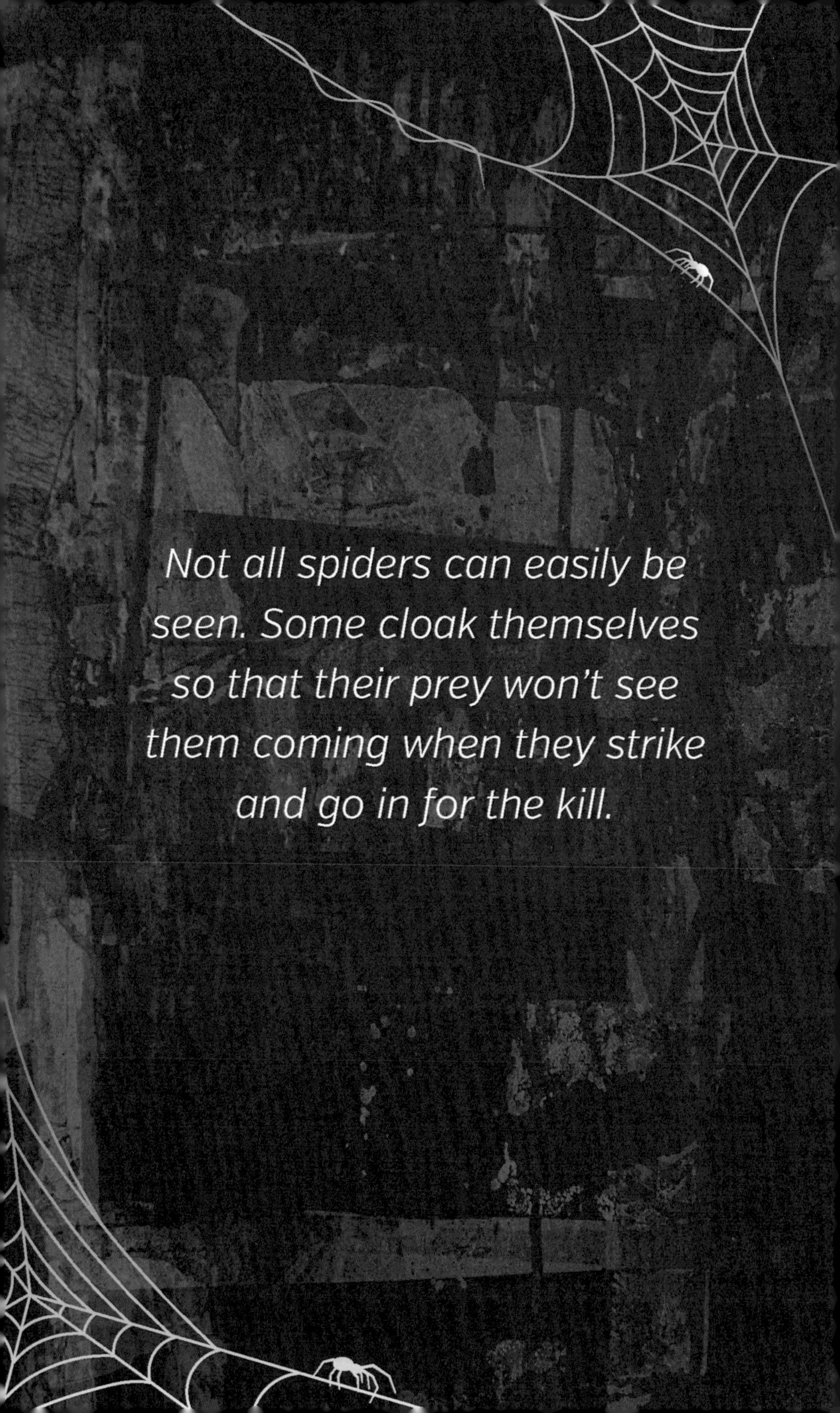

Not all spiders can easily be seen. Some cloak themselves so that their prey won't see them coming when they strike and go in for the kill.

When you truly pay attention to someone's behavior and character, the things they do and the way they move won't be a surprise. It's expected. DMX once said, "Always trust everyone to be themselves, but trust that you can see them well." Similar to a famous quote written by Maya Angelou, "When someone shows you who they are, believe them the first time." Both quotes make me question who's really at fault. Is it the people we choose to date or ourselves because many times they have shown us who they are, yet, still we put up with their disrespect and abuse?

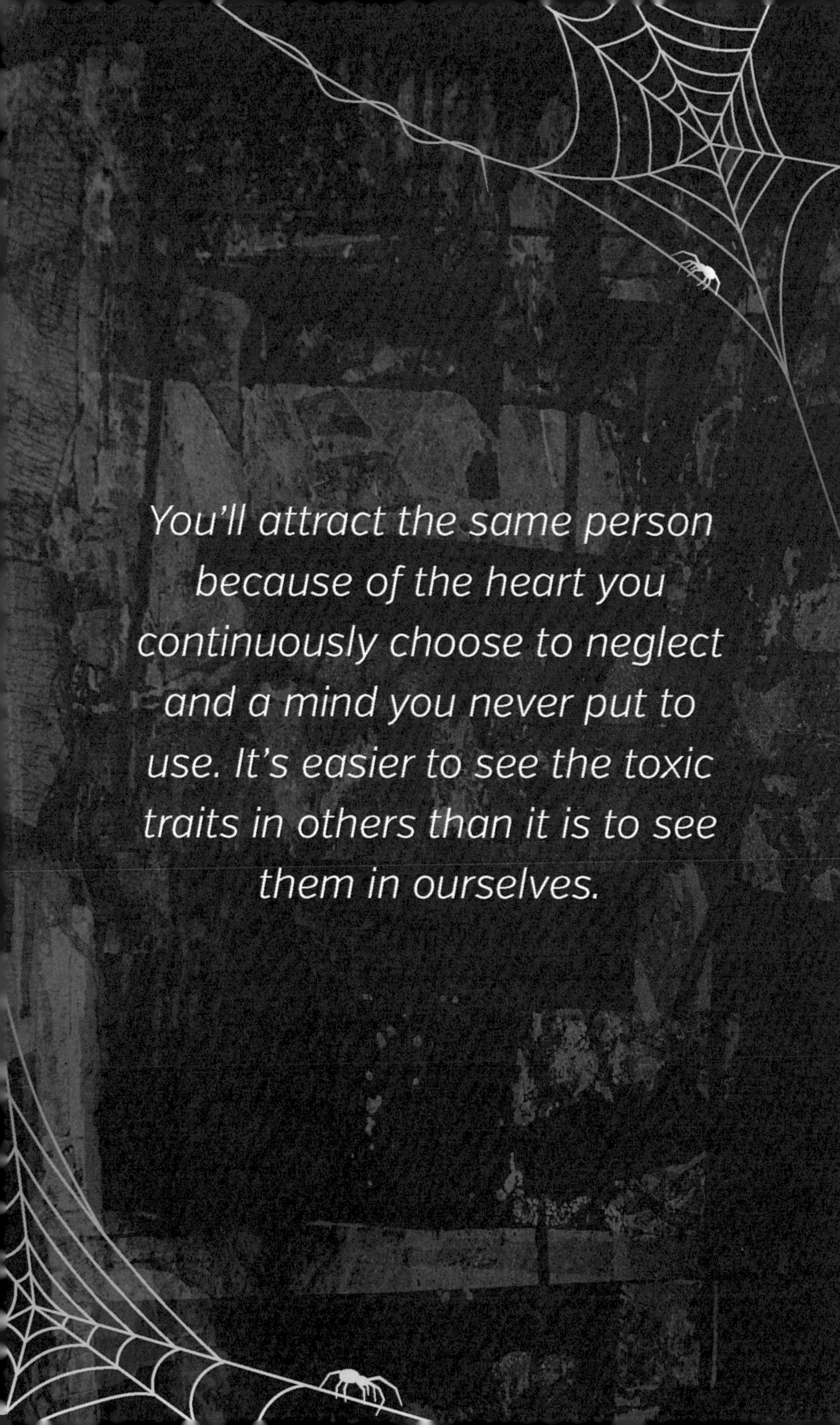

You'll attract the same person because of the heart you continuously choose to neglect and a mind you never put to use. It's easier to see the toxic traits in others than it is to see them in ourselves.

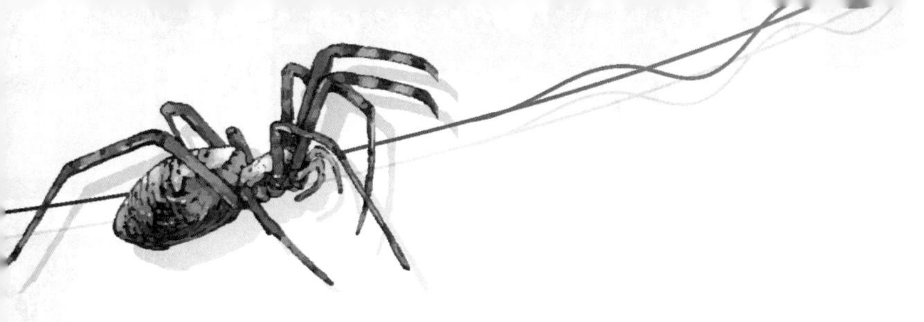

But a narcissist sees everything. They say a spider sees the world in bright images. A narcissist's vision is quite the same. They can spot your good aura from miles away. It is your good heart and high vibrational energy that attracts them to you. Running into a person with such good energy who hasn't set up healthy boundaries for themselves is like hitting a jackpot. Energy vampires they are. Like a leech, they'll search for a good way to attach themselves to you, whether mentally, emotionally, or sexually, and drain you dry. It's an energy transfer. If you ever wonder why you're always feeling depleted when you're around them, this is probably the reason.

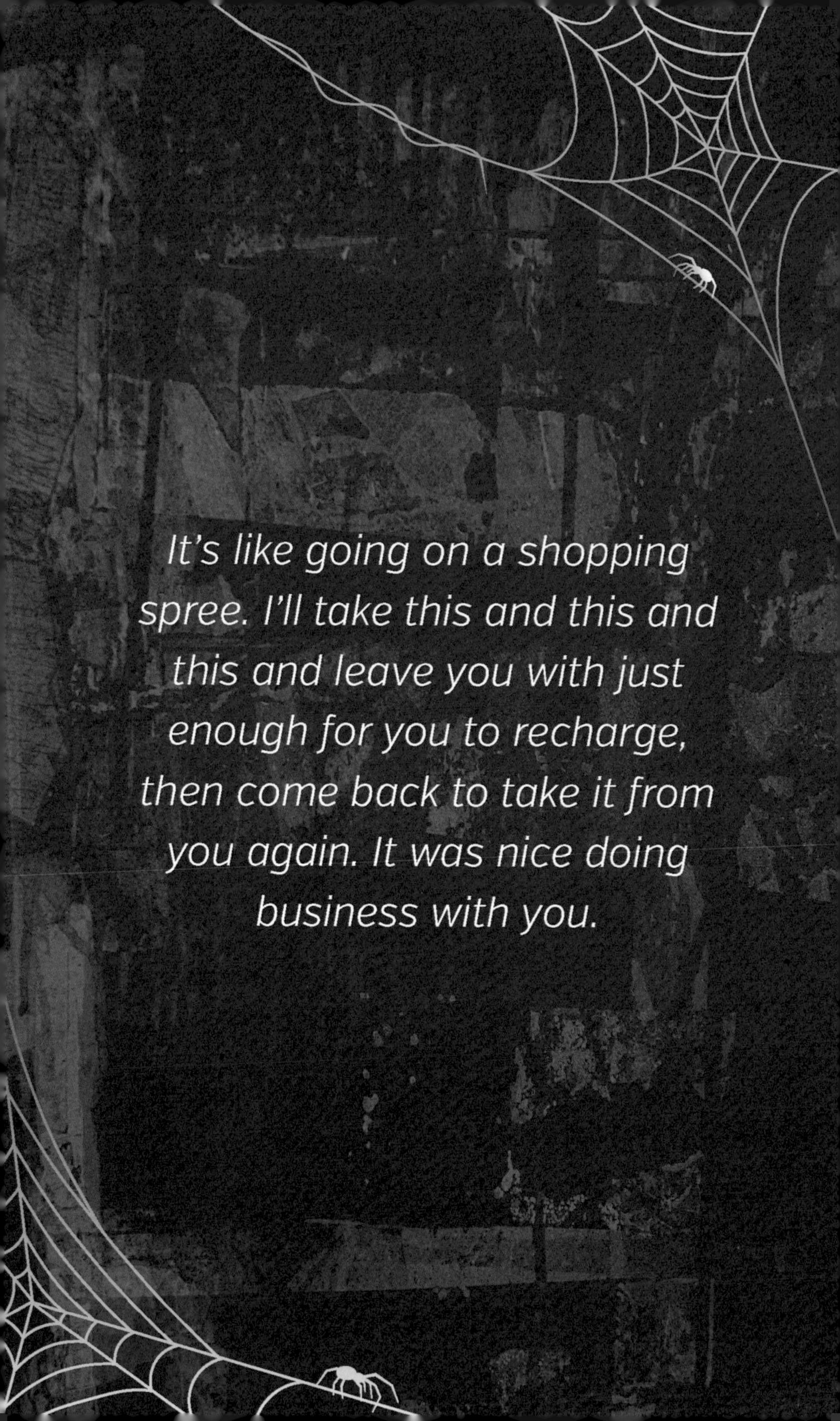

It's like going on a shopping spree. I'll take this and this and this and leave you with just enough for you to recharge, then come back to take it from you again. It was nice doing business with you.

It's a one-way street. They'll always give you the opposite of what you give to them, and if they give to you, there's always a hidden motive behind it. They'll give you just enough, but never too much. Just enough to keep you comfortable in their little web. Making it as hard as possible for you to move on. Many of us question why their victims stay, and why they don't just walk away, but it's hard to break free when you've been manipulated for years into believing it doesn't get any better than this. In addition to the emotional attachment, mental strongholds, and control they have over their victims.

They'll plant their little spider eggs of false hope inside of your mind, wait for them to hatch, then stand by and watch as their little children devour you from within. Thoughts of confusion, thoughts of unworthiness, and thoughts of fear and hopelessness. "False hope destroyed more people than love ever did."

– K. Rashad
Love Isn't Constant Pain.

If we put all of our focus on the toxic behavior of others, we will never notice our own toxic behaviors. Sometimes you have to sit back and reflect upon what lesson you are supposed to learn.There is always something to be gained in everything you go through. Whether it's a new direction you must take, a lesson to be learned, clarity, strength or wisdom. There is always something to be gained! The unhealthy relationships you've experienced with others, only mirrors back the unhealthy relationship you have with yourself. Facing your abuser is indeed hard, but facing your reflection is even harder. It forces you to see what you need to see and not what you want to see.

How can you heal your wounds if you're afraid to look at them? How can you break the toxic pattern if you don't see it? You will continue to get caught in the webs. Awareness is key. Awareness is essential! People are usually so focused on what's going on around them, but ignorant of what's going on within them. This is one of the main reasons why most people don't know what to heal or fail to notice the toxic patterns and cycles they keep repeating.

This book isn't just to be read but studied. Reflect upon all of your past or current relationships. Also, take a deeper look at the relationship you have with yourself. Healing begins when you do an honest assessment of yourself. Now that we've reached the end of this book, I want you to go back and highlight certain sections of the book that resonate with you the most. Whatever section that triggered you the most is only shedding light upon what you need to heal and should be focusing on.

I am only here to do two things: to trigger you or to inspire you, or even trigger you as I'm inspiring you. However you receive the message either or will force you to self- reflect and go within.

– K.Rashad

Are you still with me? Now pay attention, as I teach you how to move in a garden full of spiders.

The Narcissist's Web

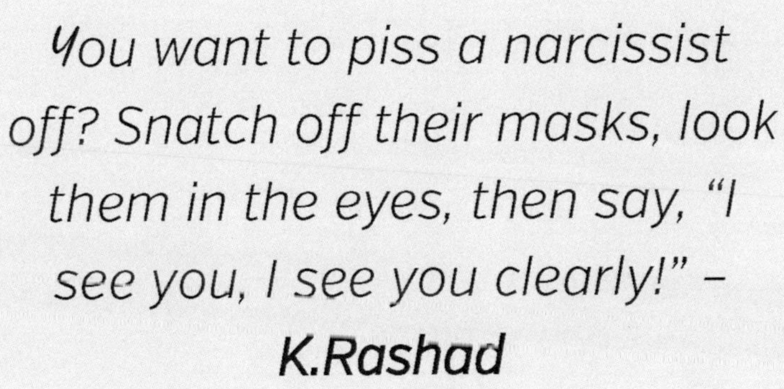
You want to piss a narcissist off? Snatch off their masks, look them in the eyes, then say, "I see you, I see you clearly!" –
K.Rashad

www.ingramcontent.com/pod-product-compliance
Ingram Content Group UK Ltd.
Pitfield, Milton Keynes, MK11 3LW, UK
UKRC031052310726
14090UKWH00028B/475

* 9 7 9 8 8 6 9 2 7 1 1 2 9 *